I0810808

The INSIDE GUIDE

GLOBAL GEOGRAPHY

Exploring South Asia's Geography

By Heather Smore

Cavendish Square

Published in 2026 by Cavendish Square Publishing, LLC
2544 Clinton Street Buffalo, NY 14224

Website: cavendishsq.com

Disclaimer: Portions of this work were originally authored by Rachael Morlock and published as *The Geography of South Asia* (Explore the World). All new material this edition authored by Heather Smore.

All websites were available and accurate when this book was sent to press.

Cataloging-in-Publication Data

Names: Smore, Heather.
Title: Exploring South Asia's geography / Heather Smore.
Description: Buffalo, NY : Cavendish Square Publishing, 2026. | Series: The inside guide: global geography | Includes glossary and index.
Identifiers: ISBN 9781502674258 (pbk.) | ISBN 9781502674265 (library bound) | ISBN 9781502674272 (ebook)
Subjects: LCSH: South Asia–Geography–Juvenile literature. | South Asia–Juvenile literature.
Classification: LCC DS336.9 S66 2026 | DDC 915.4–dc23

Editor: Katie Kawa
Designer: Deanna Lepovich

The photographs in this book are used by permission and through the courtesy of: Cover Mazur Travel/Shutterstock.com; p. 4 Pyty/Shutterstock.com; p. 6 Archi_artwork/Shutterstock.com; p. 7 sladkozaponi/Shutterstock.com; p. 8 Wirestock Creators/Shutterstock.com; p. 9 iwciagr/Shutterstock.com; p. 10 NASA images/Shutterstock.com; p. 12 (top) Robert Deller/Shutterstock.com; p. 12 (bottom) Daniel Prudek/Shutterstock.com; p. 13 Haider Jee/Shutterstock.com; p. 14 khlongwangchao/Shutterstock.com; p. 15 PhotocechCZ/Shutterstock.com; p. 16 AnupamR/Shutterstock.com; p. 17 Asif Himel/Shutterstock.com; p. 18 Dmitry Rukhlenko/Shutterstock.com; p. 19 leshiy985/Shutterstock.com; p. 20 SamanWeeratunga/Shutterstock.com; p. 21 Altug Galip/Shutterstock.com; p. 22 Ravi_Sharma1030/Shutterstock.com; p. 24 Paulo Henrique Pigozzi/Shutterstock.com; pp. 25 (top), 26 PradeepGaurs/Shutterstock.com; p. 25 (bottom) Mamunur Rashid/Shutterstock.com; p. 27 AnilD/Shutterstock.com; p. 28 (graphic organizer) Fireofheart/Shutterstock.com; p. 28 (top left) Oasis World/Shutterstock.com; p. 28 (top right) HobbitArt/Shutterstock.com; p. 28 (center) alvindom/Shutterstock.com; p. 28 (bottom left) Extezy/Shutterstock.com; p. 28 (bottom right) magr80/Shutterstock.com; p. 29 (left) Radiokafka/Shutterstock.com; p. 29 (right) zakir1346/Shutterstock.com.

CPSIA compliance information: Batch #CSCSQ26: For further information contact Cavendish Square Publishing LLC at 1-877-980-4450.

Printed in the United States of America

CONTENTS

South Asia includes these nations, as well as the Maldives.

Chapter One

WHAT IS SOUTH ASIA?

South Asia is a large geographic region, covering 2.4 million square miles (6.2 million sq km). Because of its size, it is also a very diverse geographic region, marked by a variety of landforms, waterways, and weather patterns. Exploring the countries of South Asia reveals what makes this region so unique, or special.

The Countries of South Asia

The continent of Asia is so large that it is often broken down by geographers into regions. The region of South Asia is one such division of this massive continent.

South Asia is made up of eight countries: Pakistan, India, Nepal, Bhutan, Bangladesh, Sri Lanka, the Maldives, and Afghanistan. They are the member nations of the South Asian Association for Regional Cooperation (SAARC). This organization was formed in 1985 to promote good **relationships** between the countries of this region, which are united by their geography.

Fast Fact

South Asia is part of the Asian continent, which is the largest continent on Earth.

Where Did It Come From?

South Asia is sometimes known as the Indian **subcontinent**, and it was once separated from the Asian continent by the Tethys Sea. The movement of the Indian subcontinent toward Asia happened over many millions of years, and scientists generally believe it was the result of tectonic plates shifting. Tectonic plates are pieces of Earth's crust, and they can move.

> **Fast Fact**
> The countries of South Asia are home to more than 20 percent of the world's total population.

Two plates—the Eurasian plate and the Indian plate—collided about 40 million years ago, and the Tethys Sea gradually drained. The plates continued to crunch together, lifting and folding layers of rock into mountains. This led to the formation of the Himalayas about 20 million years ago.

The Himalayas (*shown here*) formed as the Eurasian and Indian tectonic plates continued to push into each other. The Eurasian plate includes the continent of Europe and much of the continent of Asia.

South Asia's Cities

South Asia is home to around 2 billion people. Many of these people live in this region's cities, which are often very crowded and busy. New Delhi, India's capital, is one of the country's most populated cities. Another is Mumbai, which is located on India's western coast, near the Arabian Sea. These cities and their surrounding areas are each home to more than 20 million people.

Other important South Asian cities are scattered throughout the region. Dhaka is the busy capital of Bangladesh and also has a population of more than

Fast Fact

India is home to more than 1 billion people, which makes it one of the most populated countries on the planet. In fact, some sources have reported that India now has a higher population than China, which would make India the world's most populated country.

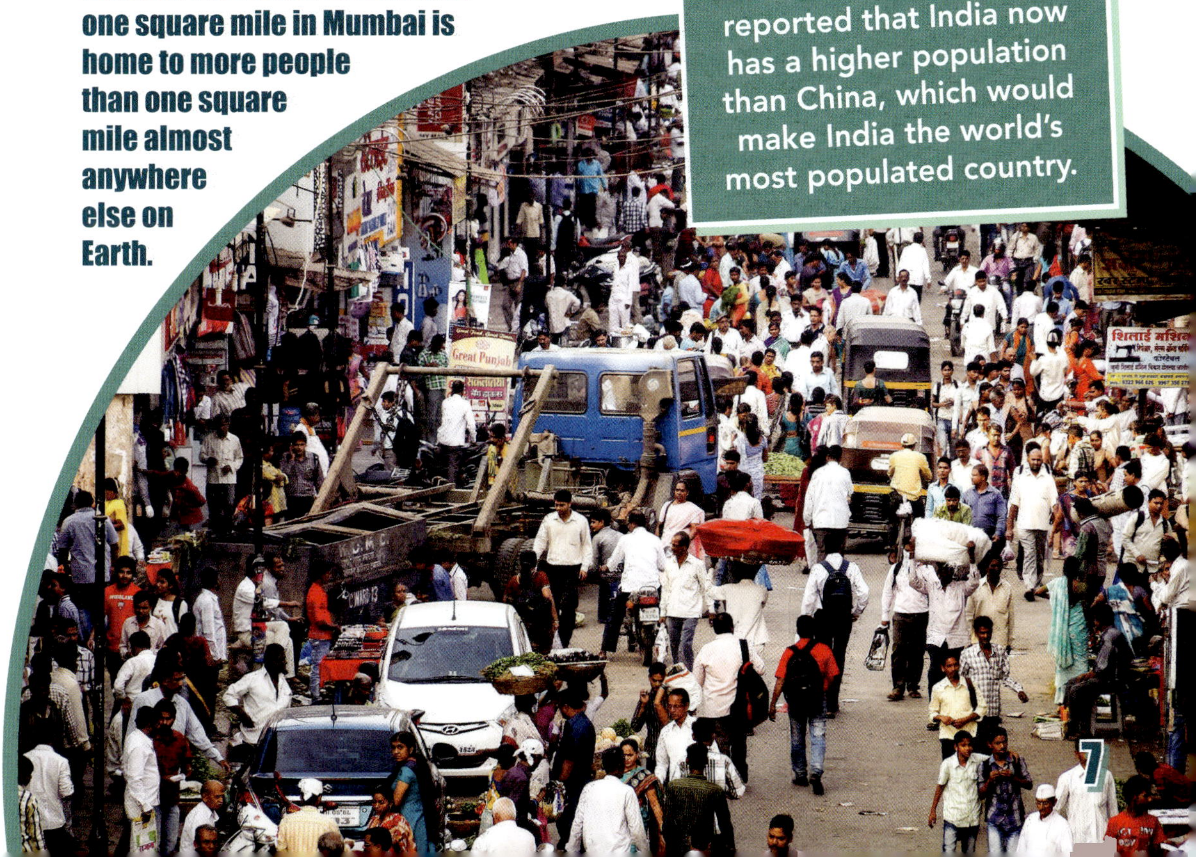

Shown here are crowds in Mumbai, which is one of the most densely populated cities in the world. This means one square mile in Mumbai is home to more people than one square mile almost anywhere else on Earth.

SOUTH ASIA'S SMALLEST CAPITAL

South Asia is home to some of the world's most crowded capital cities, but Thimphu, Bhutan, is not among them. In fact, it is the least populated capital city in South Asia. However, the capital is the largest city in Bhutan and the home of more than 100,000 people, including the country's royal family.

Thimphu is nestled into a valley in the eastern Himalayas along the Raidak River. The Raidak is a **tributary** of the Brahmaputra River that's fed by Himalayan snow and glaciers. Farmers in this valley use a method called terrace farming, growing rice and other crops on lands that can be seen from the city.

Shown here are terraces built into the hills surrounding Thimphu. Terrace farming around the capital is important for Bhutan's economy.

20 million people. Kabul is the capital city of Afghanistan. Islamabad, the capital of Pakistan, is another major city, as is Nepal's capital of Kathmandu.

A Region of Extremes

South Asia is sometimes thought of as a region of extremes. It is home to snow-capped mountains and tropical islands. Dry deserts exist in the same region as fertile river valleys. There are cities so crowded it can be hard to move around and areas so isolated it can be hard to find another person.

Perhaps the best example of the extremes of South Asia is the Himalayan mountain range. These mountains are the region's most famous geographic feature and are home to the highest peaks on Earth.

Many people looking to explore an extreme landscape head to the Himalayas.

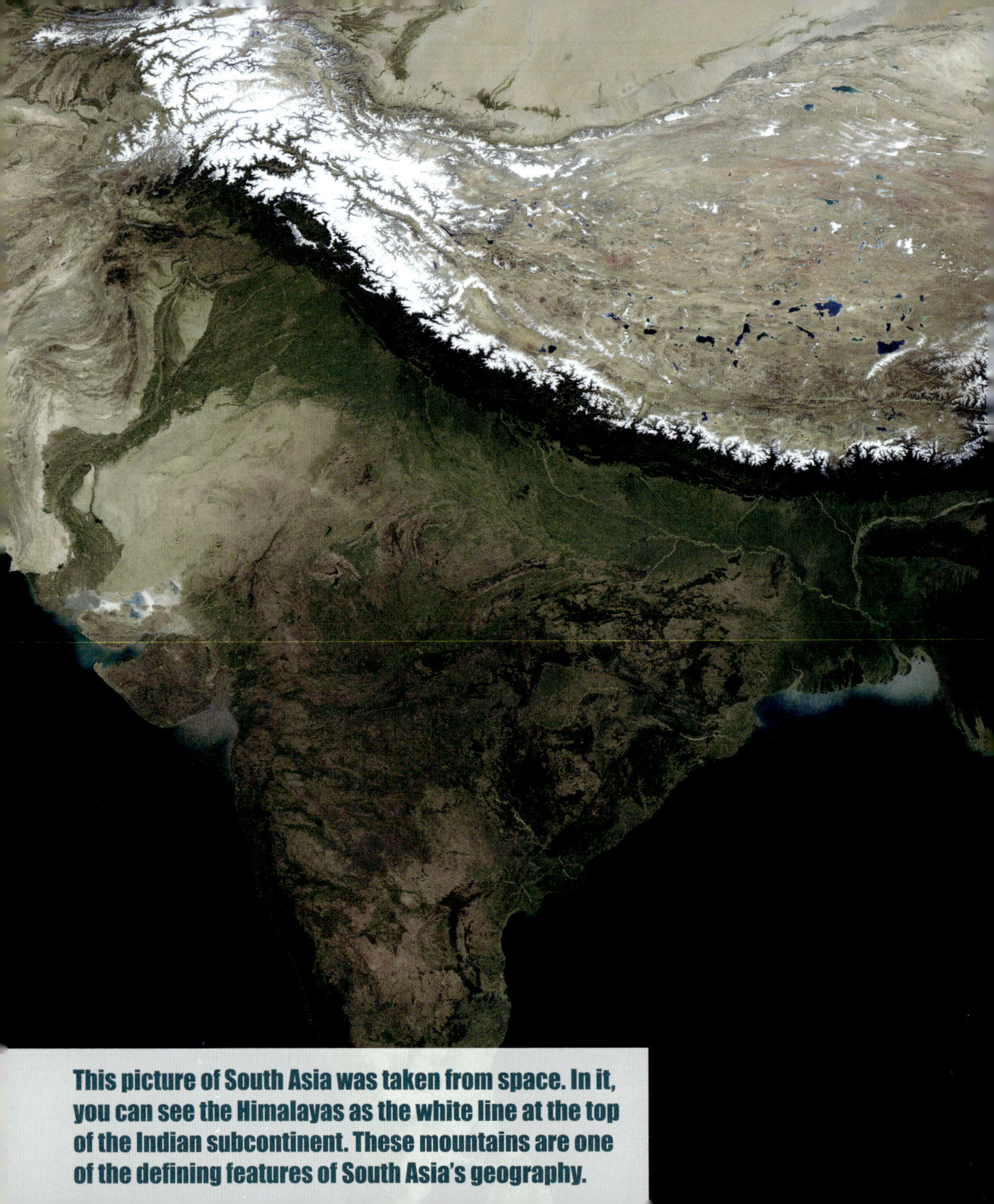

This picture of South Asia was taken from space. In it, you can see the Himalayas as the white line at the top of the Indian subcontinent. These mountains are one of the defining features of South Asia's geography.

MOUNTAINS AND RIVERS

Chapter Two

South Asia has many towering mountain ranges, and within those mountain ranges, the region's major rivers begin their paths to the sea. The most famous of these mountain ranges is the Himalayas. In addition to marking South Asia's northern boundaries, the Himalayas also influence resources and weather patterns throughout the region.

The Mighty Himalayas

The snowy peaks of the Himalayas are some of the highest in the world. These mountains cross 1,500 miles (2,414 km) from east to west and measure up to 250 miles (402.3 km) wide in places. The Himalayas pass through Afghanistan, Pakistan, India, Bhutan, and Nepal.

This mountain range hosts a variety of **ecosystems** and climates. Snow leopards, black bears, yaks, and wild goats live in higher elevations, where the temperature is often very cold. Elephants and rhinoceroses can be found in the tropical climate zones at the bases of the mountains.

Fast Fact

The name Himalaya means "abode of snow" in Sanskrit, which is a language that was used in ancient India. An abode is a home.

Pikas, such as the one shown here, are small mammals that live in the Himalayas.

Mount Everest

The Himalayas are home to the tallest mountain in the world (when only taking into account land above sea level). Mount Everest reaches a height of 29,032 feet (8,849 m) above sea level. This height was officially declared in 2020, but it's still growing! This is because

Mount Everest (*shown here*) is located on the border of Nepal and Tibet, which is a part of China in East Asia.

tectonic movements push the Himalayas up a fraction of an inch each year.

The summit of Mount Everest is **characterized** by harsh winds, freezing temperatures, and only a third of the oxygen found at sea level. These conditions make it impossible for plants or animals to survive for long. However, hundreds of climbers a year still risk their lives to reach the top of the world.

Fast Fact

In 1953, Tenzing Norgay from Nepal and Sir Edmund Hillary from New Zealand became the first documented people to reach Mount Everest's summit, or highest point.

More Mountain Ranges

The Himalayas aren't the only mountain range in South Asia. The Hindu Kush mountain range cuts through Pakistan and Afghanistan for about 500 miles (804.7 km). This range contains several important mountain passes for travel within and beyond Asia.

Glaciers in the Himalayas and Hindu Kush mountains (*shown here*) grow and melt in a yearly cycle. Meltwaters feed the mountain rivers and lakes and supply fresh water to people in the regions below.

Two mountain ranges, known as the Ghats, dominate the Indian **peninsula**. The Eastern Ghats are a series of hills alongside the east coast of the Bay of Bengal. The Western Ghats run along the coast of the Arabian Sea until the two ranges meet in the southern part of India.

Fast Fact

The Western Ghats are older than the Himalayas.

Major Rivers

The Himalayas feed three major South Asian rivers. The Indus River begins in Tibet and travels through India and into Pakistan. There, it is fed by the snow and melting glaciers of the Himalayan and Hindu Kush mountains. Then, it follows a southern course through Pakistan and empties into the Arabian Sea near the city of Karachi.

The Ganges and Brahmaputra rivers are also fed by Himalayan snow and glaciers. They begin north of the mountains and travel through deep gorges. The Ganges flows southeast through India, and the Brahmaputra hooks around Tibet and northeastern India. Both rivers flow into the Bay of Bengal after passing through Bangladesh.

The Indus River flows for 2,000 miles (3,218.7 km), making it one of the longest rivers in Asia. Its fertile valley was home to an important ancient civilization.

THE BAY OF BENGAL

In addition to the Ganges and Brahmaputra rivers, the Krishna, Godavari, Mahanadi, and Kaveri rivers also empty into the Bay of Bengal. This body of salt water is the largest bay in the world and represents the northeastern portion of the Indian Ocean. India, Bangladesh, Sri Lanka, and the Malay **Peninsula** surround the bay.

Monsoon winds affect the Bay of Bengal every year. They can cause deadly cyclones in the spring and fall. A cyclone is a tropical storm with strong winds and heavy rain.

The Ganges-Brahmaputra Delta (*shown here*) empties into the Bay of Bengal. It is the world's largest river delta, which is an area at the mouth of a river formed by deposits of mud and sand.

South Asia is home to many unique landscapes, including wetlands known as the Sundarbans. Located in the Ganges-Brahmaputra Delta, this area is known for the many plants and animals that live in and around its waters.

UNIQUE LANDSCAPES

Chapter Three

Beyond the mountains, South Asia has many other unique landscapes to explore. Geographic features such as plains, deserts, and islands make this a region of incredible natural diversity.

Fertile Farmlands

Some of South Asia's most fertile farmland can be found at the foot of the Himalayas through Pakistan, India, Nepal, and Bangladesh. This stretch of land is called the Indo-Gangetic Plain, named for the Indus and Ganges rivers. The plain was originally created from the **sedimentary** materials of the Tethys Sea.

The Indus, Ganges, and Brahmaputra river systems deposit soil, **silt**, sand, and gravel along their shores as they flow and flood. The fertile soil containing

Fast Fact

Around 14 percent of all the people on Earth live on the Indo-Gangetic Plain.

The Indo-Gangetic Plain is sometimes called South Asia's breadbasket because rice, wheat, and grains grow well in the area's rich soil. Sugarcane, maize, cotton, and other crops are also successfully grown on farmland in the area, such as the land shown here.

these deposits is called alluvium, and it's up to 6,000 feet (1,828.8 m) deep in some areas of the Indo-Gangetic Plain.

Into the Desert

Not all of the Indo-Gangetic Plain is made up of fertile farmlands. The Thar Desert is a part of the Indo-Gangetic Plain that lies mainly in northwestern India but also reaches into eastern Pakistan. It's the world's most densely populated desert and spans 77,000 square miles (199,429.1 sq km).

The Thar Desert contains sandy plains, dunes, and **sparse** plant growth. Temperatures rise in May and June, hitting up to 122 degrees Fahrenheit (50 degrees Celsius). This is also a time when seasonal dust storms hit the desert. Other South Asian deserts include the Registan Desert of Afghanistan and the Thal Desert of Pakistan.

Sand dunes such as these are a common sight in the Thar Desert.

The Deccan Plateau

Another major landform on the Indian subcontinent is the Deccan Plateau. Located south of the Thar Desert, the plateau is a very dry area of raised, flat land between the Arabian Sea and Bay of Bengal. The Eastern Ghats and Western Ghats enclose this vast plateau, which is one of the oldest geographic features of the subcontinent.

The Deccan Plateau is around 1,000 to 2,500 feet (304.8 to 762 m) above sea level. It is mostly arid, or very dry, because the Ghats protect it from monsoon winds and rain. Many people live in this area, which can cause problems for the **environment**.

Fast Fact

More than 40 percent of the Indian peninsula is covered by the Deccan Plateau.

Many ancient civilizations rose and fell on the Deccan Plateau throughout the history of South Asia. Visitors to this area today can tour ancient sites, such as the one shown here.

South Asian Islands

India's diverse geography also includes islands. The Andaman and Nicobar Islands are Indian islands near the southern coastline of Myanmar. The Andaman Islands are an archipelago, or group, of about 300 islands. The Nicobar Islands to the south include about 19 islands. Some Indigenous, or Native, groups live on these islands and avoid contact with the larger world.

Fast Fact

People only live on approximately 38 of the hundreds of Andaman and Nicobar Islands.

Sri Lanka is an island nation in the Indian Ocean near the southeastern tip of India. Its coastline includes sandy beaches and rocky cliffs. A plain makes up most of the island's area, and the plain surrounds central highlands, which are made up of plateaus and mountains.

Sri Lanka has many beautiful geographic features, including waterfalls such as the one shown here.

THE MALDIVES

The Maldives make up another South Asian island nation. They are an archipelago in the Indian Ocean, southwest of the Indian peninsula. This 510-mile (820.8 km) chain of 1,200 small islands is made of the tips of underwater volcanic mountains. The islands are clustered together into small, ring-shaped groups called atolls. About 200 of these islands are inhabited, or home to people. White sand beaches, coral reefs, and lagoons attract visitors to the Maldives. Tourism is an important part of this small nation's economy, so preserving its natural beauty is important for environmental and financial reasons.

The Maldives feature a wealth of beautiful views packed into a small amount of space. In fact, this island country is the smallest independent nation in all of Asia.

South Asia's geography has attracted many people to this region throughout history. These people adapted to the lands around them and built cities, such as New Delhi in India (*shown here*). However, the human activity in these cities has not always been good for the land.

THE ROLE OF HUMANS

Chapter Four

Humans play a very important role, or part, in shaping the geography of the regions where they live. This is certainly true in South Asia. Over time, people adapted to life in this region's extreme landscapes, and in some cases, this meant changing the land to make farming possible or to house growing populations. Lands were cleared, natural resources were used, and cities were built. These changes helped humans survive, but they often put the environment in danger.

Natural Resources

South Asia's abundance of natural resources has made it a popular place to settle since ancient times. Natural resources in this region include alluvial soil, water, forests, and minerals. About 42 percent of South Asian land is used for agriculture. Across this region, farmers grow grains like barley, corn, and wheat. Wet zones allow rice, tea, and tropical fruits to grow. Some dry zones are suited to growing dates, figs, apricots, cherries, olives, and grapes.

Fast Fact

In Bhutan, Nepal, and parts of India, hydropower—energy from moving water—is becoming a popular energy source.

Forests in South Asia contain many kinds of trees, depending on the climate. For example, pines and firs such as these grow in the highlands. In other parts of the region, teak, bamboo, and sandalwood trees grow.

Fast Fact

South Asia is rich in minerals. These include coal and iron ore from India, as well as gemstones, such as sapphires and rubies, from India and Sri Lanka.

Fresh water from snow, glaciers, and rivers supplies drinking water to large populations. Waterways are also used for **irrigation**, fishing, and transporting people and goods.

Working with the Land

Many of South Asia's geographic features once seemed like barriers to human settlement. However, humans have adapted to work with the land. Natural mountain passes have become important trade routes. In places with frequent flooding, farmers have perfected growing crops that thrive in wet environments, such as rice.

Even today, humans are continuing to develop new technologies and practices to adapt to South Asia's geography. Air conditioning systems combat heat waves, and salt is removed from drinking water through a process called desalinization, or desalination. However, the harsh environments of South Asia still present many challenges for people living in this region.

Solar energy is becoming more popular in South Asia. Solar panels, such as the ones shown here in India, take energy from the sun and use it to power factories, homes, and more. This is another way people have adapted to the environment of this region.

The Dangers of Nature

South Asia's geography has many benefits for people, but it also poses many dangers. Residents of South Asia have witnessed some of the worst natural disasters in recent history. Floods, droughts, and heat waves occur frequently in the region. Earthquakes regularly threaten the mountain ranges. Meanwhile, tsunamis are a threat to populations along the coast.

Floods are a big problem in many parts of South Asia, including Bangladesh (*shown here*). Climate change is leading to more extreme floods, as well as other weather events, such as droughts and heat waves.

In 2004, a tsunami killed more than 230,000 people, including those living in the South Asian countries of India, Bangladesh, Sri Lanka, and the Maldives. A deadly earthquake shook Nepal in 2015, displacing 2.8 million people, and another struck the country in 2023, killing more than 100 people.

Fast Fact

A tsunami is a giant ocean wave or series of waves produced by an earthquake under the water.

Facing the Future

Billions of people live in South Asia, and the land can't always support such a large population. Natural resources are sometimes stretched to their limits. In addition, large populations often lead to large amounts of pollution. This contributes to global warming and climate change.

As global temperatures rise, the Himalayan and Hindu Kush glaciers are shrinking. This is a serious problem for those who rely on these glaciers for drinking water. In addition, sea levels are rising, which can affect coastlines and islands. However, the people of South Asia are working hard to protect their part of the planet and provide hope for the future of this region.

India is the largest South Asian country in terms of both area and population. Its crowded cities produce a lot of air pollution, as shown here. Finding ways to reduce air pollution is one way Indians are working to fight climate change.

SOUTH ASIA'S MANY BIOMES

South Asia is home to many biomes, which are like neighborhoods in nature. From north to south, the climate of South Asia changes dramatically, and so do its biomes. The northern mountain highlands are cold and snowy. Around the foothills and valleys of the Himalayas in Nepal, Bhutan, and India, a humid **subtropical** zone supports a forest biome with diverse plant and animal life.

A desert biome stretches across Afghanistan, Pakistan, and northwestern India. Finally, high temperatures and heavy rainfall can be experienced in the tropical biome that includes Bangladesh, coastal stretches of India, and the southern islands of the region.

The Deccan Plateau and its surrounding areas form their own biome. This biome has a semiarid climate, which means it gets very little rainfall but still more than a desert biome.

SOUTH ASIA BY THE NUMBERS

Largest Country (by Area)

India: 1.3 million square miles (3.3 million sq km)

Most Populated Country

India: 1.4 billion people

Smallest Country (by Area)

The Maldives: 115 square miles (298 sq km)

Highest Point

Mount Everest: 29,032 feet (8,849 m)

Longest River

Indus River: 2,000 miles (3,218.7 km)

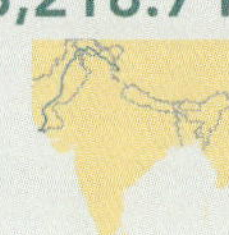

THINK ABOUT IT!

1. What geographic features do you think play a part in making South Asia one of the world's most populated regions?
2. Can you think of other parts of the world that are known as breadbaskets, like the Indo-Gangetic Plain? What do these areas have in common?
3. Throughout history, there have been many wars fought in parts of South Asia. How might wars affect the environment and geography of a region?
4. What are some ways governments, businesses, and individuals in South Asia can help protect the natural world?

GLOSSARY

characterize: To be a quality or trait of something.

ecosystem: A kind of natural community made up of all the living things in an area.

environment: The natural world around us.

irrigation: The supplying of water to land by man-made means.

monsoon: A seasonal wind, especially in the Indian Ocean and southern Asia, that affects the weather.

peninsula: A piece of land surrounded by water on three sides.

relationship: The way in which two or more people or things are connected.

sedimentary: Relating to matter such as rocks, sand, and stones that is moved and deposited by water, wind, or glaciers.

silt: Very small particles deposited by water.

sparse: Not thickly grown.

subcontinent: A major part of a continent.

subtropical: Describing a region that is very close to a tropical area.

tributary: A stream that flows into a larger stream, river, or lake.

FIND OUT MORE

Books

Davies, Monika. *India*. Minneapolis, MN: Bellwether Media, 2023.

Friesen, Helen Lepp. *India*. New York, NY: Lightbox Learning, Inc., 2023.

Morlock, Rachael. *Life and Culture in South Asia*. Buffalo, NY: PowerKids Press, 2021.

Websites

Asia: Physical Geography
education.nationalgeographic.org/resource/asia/
National Geographic presents an overview of the geography of the entire Asian continent, including South Asia.

Climate Warriors: UNICEF India
www.unicef.org/india/campaigns/climate-warriors
UNICEF is the part of the United Nations that works with young people, and this part of its website features videos from young people in India who are working to protect the environment.

Know India
knowindia.india.gov.in/
This official government website offers visitors many important facts about the land, history, and people of India.

INDEX